# Eighty Days of Faith

BY
RHONDA TOMMER

Copyright © 2013 by Rhonda Tommer

*Eighty Days of Faith*
by Rhonda Tommer

Printed in the United States of America

ISBN 9781625099426

All rights reserved solely by the author. The author guarantees all contents are original and do not infringe upon the legal rights of any other person or work. No part of this book may be reproduced in any form without the permission of the author. The views expressed in this book are not necessarily those of the publisher.

Unless otherwise indicated, Bible quotations are taken from New International Version (NIV). Copyright © 1973, 1978, 1984, 2011 by Biblica, Inc.™. Used by permission. All rights reserved.

www.xulonpress.com

# Table of Contents

*Introduction* .................................................... vii
*Dedication* ..................................................... xi
*Acknowledgements* ........................................ xiii

A New Beginning ............................................. 15
The Delivery .................................................... 25
Visiting NICU Ward 288 .................................. 28
Leaving the Hospital and Ryan ........................ 33
A New Routine ................................................ 37
Feeding Time ................................................... 42
An Encounter with a Tall, Dark Stranger ........ 44
Jimmy Takes a Turn for the Worse .................. 46
Ryan is Moved ................................................. 49
Holding Ryan for the First Time ..................... 52
Ryan the Fighter .............................................. 55
Ryan, Can you Find Mommy? ......................... 57

Taking a Day to Myself . . . . . . . . . . . . . . . . . . . . . . . . . . . . . 59

Bottle Feeding – Suck, Swallow, *Breathe* . . . . . . . . . . . . . . . . . . . 63

Growing in Grace and Size . . . . . . . . . . . . . . . . . . . . . . . . . . . 65

Faith Beyond Eighty Days. . . . . . . . . . . . . . . . . . . . . . . . . . . . 73

*Photo Gallery*. . . . . . . . . . . . . . . . . . . . . . . . . . . . . . . . . . . 87

# INTRODUCTION

*I* started writing *"Eighty Days of Faith"* in 2005, after attending a five-week writing class. The only assignment for the class was to write something and submit it to the teacher on the fourth week. We would get it back with the instructor's comments on week five. I have always wanted to chronicle my son's premature birth and his 80-day hospital stay. I have always had his story rolling around in my head. So, I started writing. By the fourth week I had the working title and the first chapter of what would become the book that you hold in your hand.

The night the educator returned the students' "masterpieces" he started on the opposite side of the room from where I sat. He had written comments and marked up everyone's papers. I could see a lot of writing on other students' papers. He gave verbal comments to each student as he handed them their writings. I heard things like, "You need to complete your sentences." "There are too many grammatical errors." Or, "Your story doesn't show enough feeling." "It doesn't flow well."

I couldn't wait to see how he would criticize my work. I was thinking, "This is my story." He can't possibly know the emotion I poured into this first chapter, and I was concerned that he was going to "unwrite" it. He handed it to me, looked me straight in the eye and said, "It's on a very rare occasion that I return a student's paper without finding something negative to say about it.

This is a great start. You should finish the book."

The only thing he wrote on my paper, besides a response to a comment I made about gaining so much weight during my pregnancy, was "<u>Good</u> work-it could be tightened. Well done, mechanically." Needless to say, I was thrilled and encouraged.

This was the first writing class I had ever taken outside of what was required to graduate from high school. My so-called writing experience started in the early 1980s when I reluctantly inherited the job of writing and editing the company newsletter for Fedco Department Stores. I was employed there during most of the 1980s. That experience was what got me hired for my next job, even though my official title was administrative assistant to the personnel manager. I've also produced newsletters for many clubs and non-profit organizations over the years. I also write a monthly opinion column for a local newspaper.

After the five-week class, I took some communications classes at Dixie State College in Southern Utah to improve my writing skills. I was never sure this story would ever leave my computer. It was therapy for me to write. It wasn't until 2013 that my therapy would turn into a book.

My desire was to share our eighty-day hospital experience with others and explain how God touched our lives with this little miracle. End of story. But that is not the end of the story, and to stop there didn't fulfill my goal of encouraging other parents of preemies. To truly encourage parents and share the miracle, I needed to share how God has worked in our son's life after leaving the hospital; I needed to include part two of *Eighty Days*.

So, at the end of our eighty days of hospital stay you will find part two. Doctors told us Ryan could be a delayed learner, a sickly child, and could have motor skill issues as he grew up. Did this actually happen? You will have

## Introduction

to read part two, which I call *Faith Beyond Eighty Days,* to find out.

It is my prayer that you will be uplifted and encouraged by this book. Each of us will struggle with difficulties that will require faith to see us through. As the Israelites wandered the desert for forty years, trusting that God would bring them to the Promised Land, we will wander through these difficult days, sometimes full of doubt and sometimes full of hope, as we trust that God's plan is always the best plan, and His timing is never too late, nor never too soon, and always perfect.

# Dedication

Ryan, I dedicate this book to you.
You have taught me so much.
your positive attitude;
your insatiable desire to learn;
your unending sense of humor and wit;
your care and concern for others;
all point to your dedication to live out your life
in a constant quest to be the man that God created you to be.
Thank you, Ryan, for bringing your father and me so much joy.
Thank you for being a loving son and big brother, and such an
integral part of this family.
I love you, son.

Mom

# Acknowledgements

This book would not have been made possible if not for the encouragement of my family and friends to see it to completion. I'd like to thank my husband, Mike, for constantly encouraging me to work on my book. I'd like to thank my friend, Jessica Blevins, for editing the first part of my book and giving me some good advice regarding watching my tenses. I'd like to thank Margie Black, my mom and Sharon Kearney, my aunt for conducting a final edit and giving me good ideas on how to improve. I'd especially like to give thanks to God for seeing me through to the final product, for His unstoppable grace and for always being there to remind me to keep the faith.

# A New Beginning

*Jesus replied, "I tell you the truth, if you have faith and do not doubt, not only can you do what was done to the fig tree, but also you can say to this mountain, 'Go, throw yourself into the sea,' and it will be done.*

*Matthew 21:21*

April 11, 1990. This was the day that we would bring our newborn son, now almost three months old, home from the hospital. I have been waiting for this time for eighty days, but somehow, I didn't feel like I was ready. The nurses at the hospital said I was ready; my husband, Mike and my mom said that I was ready. But what would I do without a whole staff of doctors and nurses around if I needed them? They had been there since the day my son was born.

I called early in the morning to make sure that we were still on schedule. After all, there had been at least two occasions in which he was scheduled to come home, but was not able to because of some "minor setback." The first time he experienced a rapid weight gain, which indicated that he was retaining fluid. The second time he was running low grade fever, indicating that he may have an infection of some type. But today, at least for this moment, our little guy was given the A-OK to come home.

As I was deciding which of my "fat clothes" to put on for the joyous occasion, I again started kicking myself for gaining so much weight. How could I gain sixty pounds only to give birth to a two pound, six ounce baby? What was I thinking? I thought about how many times I would walk across the street from where I worked as an administrative assistant and order not one, but two hot dogs for lunch - one for me and one for the baby. Lesson learned: unborn babies do not need hot dogs.

I really enjoyed my job, and when I delivered so unexpectedly at twenty-seven weeks gestation, my boss, Jeff Stanger, was so understanding and compassionate. I took my maternity leave until it was all gone, contemplating going back to work until our son could come home. But when the time came to return to work or put in my notice, I knew that God's plan was for me to be a stay-at-home mom. Jeff graciously and understandingly accepted my resignation.

After finally deciding what to wear to the hospital, Mike and I ate a quick breakfast, made sure the base of the infant car seat was property installed in the car and started our trek to the hospital one last time. Mom joined us for the joyous occasion, with video camera in the ready.

During the twenty-six mile ride to Long Beach Memorial Medical Center/Miller Children's Hospital from our Home in La Habra, California, I contemplated the last eighty days of my life, and the first eighty days of this baby's life. He just didn't come into this world the way babies are supposed to. He had a rough start. During the first seventy-two hours of his life, his doctors would not give us any guarantee what-so-ever that he would survive. After three days, his survival rate went up to 30 percent and slowly progressed the longer he lived. Those were the longest three days of my life.

# A New Beginning

A week before an emergency C-section Mike and I had gone to our favorite place, Laguna Lake Park in Fullerton, California, to feed the ducks. It was so peaceful there, and everything was right on track. It was a cool January day. There were not very many people there on that day. There was the occasional runner and a couple of people riding their horses on the trail along the lake.

We visited our favorite breakfast spot, Robert's Coffee Shop, for the best pancakes west of the Mississippi. After breakfast we stopped at the day-old bakery to buy the cheap bread at ten loaves for a dollar. We took the camera and took pictures for the photo album I started to chronicle the baby's life from the time I knew I was pregnant until birth.

When we discovered that I was pregnant in September of 1989, I was anxious for the first trimester of my pregnancy. I had a miscarriage in December of 1987, during my twelfth week of pregnancy. I thought if I could just get through those first three months, everything would be fine. Now, here I was at the park, twenty-six weeks along, and everything was going as planned.

We had toured the soon-to-be-opened maternity ward at Friendly Hills Medical Center, right up the street from our house. It was scheduled to open in April of 1990. The timing couldn't be more perfect. My due date was April 18, and the baby would be born in a brand new, state-of-the-art maternity ward. Maybe it would even be written up in the paper for being the first baby born in the new ward.

A few days following our visit to the duck park, as we called it, I started having cramps. They felt like menstruation cramps at first, but started getting stronger as time went on. I scheduled an appointment to see my doctor, and he increased my calcium intake. The cramps had not subsided after a couple of more days, and Mike took me to the emergency room at Whittier Hospital, since that is where Friendly Hills doctors were delivering babies while waiting for their new maternity ward to open. It just so happened that my obstetrician, Dr. Arman, was on duty when we arrived there. He examined me and suggested that I stay the night for observation. I was transferred to a room and placed on an external fetal monitor for the night.

Late in the night my doctor's replacement came in to see how I was doing. Dr. Bloom checked the monitor and said that everything looked good. She said that she would consider releasing me, but that Dr. Arman had written in my chart not to release me until morning. I was scared and upset. Dr. Bloom pulled a chair up to my bed and spent a lot of time calming my fears. She reassured me that, if there were going to be problems with the baby, I was exactly where I needed to be. After she left my room in the wee hours of the morning, I was finally able to get some sleep.

Around seven in the morning Dr. Barnett came in to check things out. He had relieved Dr. Bloom earlier that morning. He checked the monitor and said that no contractions had been recorded. He said that he would be back to examine me and, if everything looked good, I could go home. I was a bit nervous because I was still feeling the cramps that I had come in for. I called Mike at home and told him the news. He said that he was going to Scotty's Restaurant, a quaint little coffee shop in Whittier owned by some dear friends of ours, for breakfast on his way to pick me up.

Dr. Barnett returned a few minutes later and examined me. He looked up at me and said, "You've dilated two centimeters!" After he said that, there was a whirlwind of activity. Nurses came in and started an IV. They put me on a medication called Slo-Mag to try to stop the contractions, which we learned could only be recorded by an internal fetal monitor.

All I could do was pray, "Oh God, please don't bring us this far to let this happen! Please don't let this baby die!" I heard Dr. Barnett on the phone outside of my room. He was saying something like, "...whatever you can get here first, ambulance or helicopter, it don't matter to me." He then came in and told me that I was being transported to Long Beach Memorial Medical Center/Miller Children's Hospital for care. The Slo-Mag was doing its job, and I was shivering as if I was freezing, but at the same time, I was burning hot. I felt like I was lying on a bed of fire.

I remembered the word helicopter and promptly informed Dr. Barnett that these feet were not leaving the ground. I would not fly in a helicopter. He smiled and said, "We'll just see what gets here first." I tried to call Mike, but he had already left for the restaurant. I knew that Dr. Barnett would not wait for him to get to the hospital, so I had to get in touch with him.

I called my mom and told her what was going on. She had already talked to Mike that morning and got the news that I was being released. How quickly things had changed. She called Mike at Scotty's and then headed to the hospital herself. Mike arrived at the hospital just in time to jump into the ambulance with me.

I was practically hysterical as I was being wheeled to the ambulance through the emergency room. One of the nurses who had been caring for me stopped my gurney, looked me straight in the eyes, and said, "You need to stop this! You and your baby are going to the best hospital around. If the baby comes early, it has a very good chance of surviving and living a normal life. I've seen babies born earlier than yours, and they are doing fine. You've got to have faith!" I knew in my heart that this nurse had a very strong faith in God. I knew she was trying to connect with me on a spiritual level without sounding religious. She did.

Once in the ambulance, me in the back and Mike in the front, we started our 26 mile trip to Long Beach. Little did we know that this would be one of some eighty plus trips we would make before our baby would come home. They had to stop the Slo-Mag IV for the ride because I was under the care of two EMTs and not a nurse. I was thankful for that, but my thanks were short lived because the IV started again the minute I reached a room at the hospital.

Once I was settled in, we met Dr. Harding. I would be under his care for the night. I told him right off, as he was performing an ultrasound that we didn't want to know if the baby was a boy or a girl. He smiled and turned the screen away from my view, like I could actually tell what was on there anyway.

Dr. Harding did several ultrasounds throughout the night. At one point he would refer to the baby as "she". The next time he would come in and say that "he" was holding his own. This became comic relief between the two of us. At one point he even said "they" were doing well. His easy going manner helped me to relax.

Dr. Harding had the nurse administer a steroid through my IV that was intended to speed up the development of the baby's lungs. He said for the medication to do its job, it needed to be in my system at least twelve hours. That would put our estimated time of delivery at about 4:00 a.m., if we could hold the baby off that long.

Mike really wanted the baby to be born on Sunday, the Lord's Day, if he was to be born premature. I understood his thinking. Mike's father died on a Sunday, after a month-long stay in the hospital. His mother suffered a heart attack on Easter Sunday in April of 1983. She passed away three days later. He once said that nothing like that should happen on the Lord's Day. Sundays were special. They should be filled with joy.

I was hoping the baby would be born in April as planned. But it didn't look like that was going to happen. At this point Dr. Harding was just trying to hold off as long as possible.

The Slo-Mag was wearing me down. I was burning up. I needed water. Dr. Harding nixed that idea, because I could possibly be going into surgery. He informed me that the baby was breach, and I would have to have a Caesarean Section. The baby would not survive a vaginal birth. Because I would be going into surgery I could not drink any water or have anything to eat.

I was so hot, yet I was shivering like I was cold. Every time someone came into the room, they would try to cover me up. But I'd kick the sheet off because it felt hot to the touch. I finally convinced Dr. Harding to allow me to rinse my mouth out with water and not swallow it. He made me promise not to swallow the water. About every fifteen minutes I would yell, "RINSE!", and whoever was in the room at the time would put a straw up to my lips so I could take a sip of water and spit it out. Mom was there to give us moral support. Dad came as soon as he heard that I had been transferred.

Early that morning, which was a Saturday, Dad delayed going to his golf tournament until he heard that I was coming home. Then he left for his tournament and could not be reached. This was before the days of a cell phone in every purse or pocket. And pagers were used only during the work day.

Mike, Mom and Dad would come into my darkened room one or two at a time to check on me. If they were not in my room when I loudly requested a rinse one of them would come running. I also made frequent requests to use my dad's *ChapStick*. My lips were so dry, and I knew I could count on Dad to have a *ChapStick* in his pocket. I was so glad when he arrived at the hospital.

Sometime in the early evening, around seven, my grandparents came by from Whittier. I knew this was a long journey for them because they didn't take the freeways. Instead they drove side streets all the way to Long Beach. That was the only way they knew how to come. I was so glad to see my grandma. But she was so upset and crying, filled with fear and worry over what was going to happen. She got me upset after I had spent so much time trying to calm myself down and think positive. After she left my room, I told Mom, "Mom, I love Grandma but please don't let her come back in here. I don't have enough faith for both of us right now."

Around midnight, Dr. Harding came into my room, did the umpteenth examination and quietly announced that it was time to deliver the baby. I had dilated to six centimeters, and he did not want me to start to deliver the baby naturally. He needed to perform the C-section before nature took over. He said that the baby would be "small and have to stay in the hospital for a while." In my mind, that translated into about five pounds and perhaps a couple of weeks. Nothing prepared me for the trial we were about to face.

I always thought that I was in control of every circumstance. Before accepting Christ as my Savior, I thought I was "Charles in charge." Mike did a good job at letting me think that.

Though I was raised in church until I was old enough to say I didn't want to go anymore, I never really had that personal relationship with Christ. In October of 1987 God changed that. October 1, 1987 is when God showed me that I really was not in control.

On that Thursday morning I was pulling into the parking lot at Fedco Department Stores' main office in Santa Fe Springs, California. It was early, a good half an hour before most employees start arriving, and the lot was nearly empty.

Just as I made my right turn in the parking lot my car started rocking. I stopped in the driveway as the shaking continued. The DJ on the radio announced that we were having an earthquake. "If you're in your car, stay there. If you're in a building find cover." He was barking out instructions and I remember thinking this guy is calm. I would be yelling something foolish like, "Oh, my God. We are all gonna die!"

As I looked over the parking lot I could see waves under the pavement and I saw ripples in it as if I were standing on the shore looking over the ocean. I parked my car and got out just as the shaking stopped. Another employee met me and we hugged one another for a long moment, each seeking comfort from the other.

I realized at that moment that I might be able to control the little things in my life, but I had no control over the things that really mattered. I spent the next several days living in fear as major aftershocks rocked my world.

The quake, centered in Whittier, was just a couple of miles north of me. It registered 5.9 on the Richter scale. Two days after the main quake, at about 4:00 in the morning, a 5.6 magnitude aftershock struck, leaving us in the dark. I was terrified.

I skipped work on the following Monday and Tuesday. But I was afraid to stay home by myself, so Mike would drop me off at my grandparents' house like I was a child in need of a babysitter. Suddenly, this girl who was so cool, so strong, so in control couldn't even control her own emotions.

While at my grandparents' I listened to a cassette tape of my two uncles, Kenny and David, singing gospel songs. I listened to it over and over as I moved about the house so I couldn't feel the frequent aftershocks. My grandma would talk to me about how I need to put my faith in God. He was the only one bigger than an earthquake and bigger than my fears.

On Tuesday, October 6, 1987, four days after the earthquake I found myself alone in the house. Mike had gone out back. I couldn't be alone in the house! I had to get out the back door. As I raced through the living room to the back door my Bible caught my eye. It had a prominent place on the coffee table. It was occasionally dusted, but rarely opened.

I stopped, picked it up, sat down in the rocker and started reading. I read about disasters, earthquakes, famines, war and rumors of war. As I flipped through the pages, my eyes fell to Philippians 4:6-7, which reads, "Don't worry about anything; instead, pray about everything; tell God your needs and don't forget to thank him for his answers. If you do this you will experience God's peace, which is far more wonderful than the human mind can understand. His peace will keep your thoughts and your hearts quiet and at rest as you trust in Christ Jesus." (The Living Bible)

Peace! That's what I needed. Peace that goes beyond my own understanding. I knelt down at the rocker, in the quietness of my living room and asked Jesus to take control of my life. I gave him my fear. I would like to say that I was instantaneously free from fear and worry. But old habits die hard. Over time, as I grew in my relationship with the Lord, I learned to give him the big things. And he let me think I was handling the small things.

What I was facing now, trying not to go into preterm labor, was definitely one of the big things. I was in a situation that I needed to hand over to God. The only part that I could control was my own attitude. After I gave God the whole situation, in the quiet darkness of my hospital room, I could settle down a bit and I knew that, regardless of the outcome, God would see us through this crisis.

# The Delivery

*For you created my inmost being; you knit me together in my mother's womb.*

*Psalm 139:13*

At about 1:00 a.m. on January 21, 1990, I was wheeled down to the pre-op room so that an epidural could be started. This was three hours before the steroid would have its full effect on the baby's lungs.

I was very weak and unable to keep my back straight so the anesthesiologist could do his job. Eventually, he became irritated with me and told me that I had to sit up straight and be still. He angrily explained that he could not perform his task without my cooperation. Eventually, I was able to comply and I started losing sensation from my chest down.

Between Mike and Mom, it was decided that Mom would be the one to witness this blessed, however scary, event. Dad's job was to sit with Mike in the waiting room. Once I was satisfactorily numb, I was taken into the surgical room. Even though it was the middle of the night, I felt like I was lying in the light of day. A whole team of doctors and nurses were moving about the room, getting ready for a premature delivery.

Once I was prepped Mom was brought in and instructed to stand at my head. A sheet had been erected to prevent her from observing the actual surgery. But I could see what was going on by looking at the two-inch wide circular metal edge around the surgical light overhead. It took me a while to realize that I was actually watching the doctor's scalpel on my skin.

When the baby was delivered, he was whisked away by a team of doctors and nurses. Just before he left the room, I heard what sounded like the cry of a newborn kitten. I didn't realize that it was actually the baby until Mom asked, "Did you hear him cry?" She asked the doctor if it was a boy or a girl. He was busy putting me back together and he looked up at us and said, "I forgot to look." He yelled to the nurses who were tending to the baby, and said, "It's a boy!"

I lay there, waiting several minutes for them to place my newborn son in my waiting arms before I realized that he wasn't even in the room anymore. He was now the critical patient. I was sent down to recovery, where I spent the rest of the night, alone with my thoughts.

Mike came in a couple of hours after the surgery and said that he got to see our baby boy. He said he looked great, and he would be fine. In my mind he was a healthy, normal baby. I still hadn't grasped exactly what we would be facing for the next several months. Mike told me to start thinking about a name, kissed me on the forehead and headed home for some much needed sleep.

Our son was born at 1:47 a.m., on Sunday, January 21, 1990, three months short of his April 18 due date. He weighed approximately two pounds and six ounces, or 1090 grams in "nurse talk." Sunday, it was the Lord's Day.

Once I could feel my feet, I was taken to a room which I shared with another mom who delivered a preemie. We hit it off pretty good, and made an agreement to walk down to the neonatal intensive care unit as soon as we both felt up to it, to introduce ourselves to our new babies.

# Visiting NICU Ward 288

*He has made everything beautiful in his time, He has also set eternity in the hearts of men; yet they cannot fathom what God has done from beginning to end.*

*Ecclesiastes 3:11*

After several hours of rest, my roommate and I decided it was time to take that long walk down to the nursery. We decided to push a wheel chair along in case one of us needed to rest. It was the longest walk I've ever taken. Once there, we separated to go meet our babies for the first time.

Nothing prepared me for what I was about to experience. No one told me what to expect. In my mind's eye, I saw a "normal" nursery with "normal" babies, not a room full of complicated machines, pinging sounds and isolets; babies with tubes and wires coming from everywhere.

It just so happened that my baby was right by the door. I spotted the name "Tommer" on his isolette. The shock that I felt inside must have been all over my face, because his nurse immediately said, "You must be Mom."

Nurse Pam Schwene started explaining to me everything that was happening to my son. I flashed back to a memory of when I was a little girl and found a baby bird that had fallen out of its nest. It had no feathers, and lived only for a few hours after I placed it in a shoe box and gave it some water in a plastic lid to a butter container.

The baby was lying on his stomach with his knees tucked up underneath him in a fetal position. He had no diaper on. I could see every vein in his back and arms because his skin was so thin. He had a wire attached to an IV called a femoral cut down, in which a catheter had been inserted through the groin into a main artery for administering medication by intravenous distribution. This was the only vein big enough to handle a needle, and it was considered major surgery for one so small.

The baby was given morphine to calm his premature nervous system. He was given Aminophyllin to keep him from falling asleep too soundly and stop breathing. Pam explained that it was similar to getting pure caffeine. He was placed on a ventilator to help him breath. His eyes were covered with cotton strips to protect them from the bili light that was being used to control the jaundice caused by an under-developed liver. He had a red light taped to his foot to monitor the oxygen saturation in his blood. This became known as his "heart light".

This first visit did not go well. Pam asked if I would like to touch him. "No! I can't let myself get attached," I responded. I was terrified at what I saw. I started crying and asked to be taken back to my room. My nurse was called to wheel me back to my room in the wheel chair that my roommate and I had brought down with us to NICU. I got a brief scolding along the way for leaving my room without permission.

Not long after my field trip to the NICU my bedside phone rang. I was in a drug-induced, sleepy state due to the pain medications I had been given. When I answered the phone the woman at the end sounded strange, no one

I recognized. She introduced herself and explained that she was the mother of a preemie who was then three years old.

I suddenly took a great interest in what she had to say. She was part of a parent support group. Her mission was to give me encouragement. Her story frightened me. She explained that she had given birth to twins. Immediately I started shooting questions at her. How old is your baby now? What kinds of health issues is she dealing with? What do I have to look forward to?

She started explaining her experience. She had a condition called Twin to Twin Transfusion Syndrome (TTTS). This is an imbalance in blood flow between the two babies. There is a transfer of blood from one twin to the other, leaving one baby (known as the donor) with an unhealthy blood flow and the other baby (the receiver) with a healthy blood flow. This results in one baby growing in the womb, and the other starving.

When this woman's babies were born, the larger one had a life-threatening illness. Even though she received more nutrition before birth, she didn't survive. The smaller baby, named Emily weighed just over three pounds. At three years old she had hearing and vision problems and she was still on oxygen.

This was not what I needed to hear after visiting my son for the first time. I was angry at the women for calling me. I was overwhelmed with fear. I was also angry at God for letting this happen to my son. I cried myself back to sleep.

Today babies with TTTS have a much better chance of survival due to a procedure called fitoscopic laser intervention. The survival rate for one twin is 85 percent, and for both twins it's about 60 percent. Medical advances have come a long way in the past 20 years.

Mike came to the hospital late that afternoon. I was angry with him for waiting so long to come back. I didn't take into account that he was at the hospital until about 4:00 a.m. He was in need of sleep. And he was dealing with his own doubts and fears. But Mike never for one minute thought that our son would not make it. He said the first time he saw our new baby boy early that morning he knew that everything would be okay. He said that the look in his son's face when he looked at his daddy for the first time reassured Mike that we would all be okay. I had to lean on Mike's faith, because at that moment I had none of my own.

Mike suggested that we name the baby Ryan Michael. He picked Ryan after Nolan Ryan, pitcher for the Texas Rangers at the time. Nolan Ryan was in his mid forties, and was still pitching. Mike considered him an underdog because announcers talked about Nolan Ryan like he was a has-been, an old timer. But he proved his critics wrong time and again. Mike identified our Ryan with Nolan Ryan, saying that he's going to prove everyone wrong and fight to survive. He was right.

After Ryan came home from the hospital, we mailed Nolan Ryan one of the birth announcements. We couldn't believe it when we received an autographed baseball from Nolan Ryan and a letter from his wife. It arrived in nine by thirteen inch envelope with the Texas Rangers logo on it. It was a miracle that it even made it to the house. Anyone could tell just by looking at the envelope that it had a baseball in it.

Once Mike arrived at the hospital, and I got over my mad spell, he wheeled me back down to the NICU to visit our son. This time I knew exactly what to expect, and I was prepared. When Pam asked me if I wanted to touch him, I said yes. But first, the three minute scrub and a gown. I could only touch his hand because of his extremely sensitive nervous system. Any touch or bright light caused the baby to startle and jump.

Pam explained that she would be Ryan's primary nurse throughout most of his stay at the hospital. She explained all the tubes and wires, and what the purpose of each one was. Ryan was in unit 288, where the most critical babies stayed. The patient to nurse ratio was one to one. There were three different units in the NICU.

When we left Ryan's bedside we looked around in the other units at other babies. We realized that our situation was not unique. There were babies even smaller than ours. To get to the Neonatal Intensive Care Unit, we had to pass the nursery where the full term babies were on display. After spending time in the NICU, the babies in the newborn nursery looked so big. Walking into NICU was like stepping into a different world.

# Leaving the Hospital... and Ryan

*Do not be anxious about anything, but in everything, by prayer and petition, with thanksgiving, present your requests to God. And the peace of God, which transcends all understanding, will guard your hearts and your minds in Christ Jesus.*

*Philippians 4:6-7*

On Monday afternoon, just one day after Ryan's birth, Dr. Harding came in to see how I was doing. He examined me, asked how I was feeling and announced that I would probably be able to go home the next morning. I could tell that Dr. Harding thought that I would be happy to hear his news. The stubborn four-year-old that lives quietly inside me most of the time jumped at the chance of rebellion.

"I'm not leaving this hospital without my son," I stated. Dr. Harding tried to reason with me by telling me how my baby needed a lot of care. It would be weeks, maybe even months before he would be able to come home. Dr. Harding said that he doubted that I would want to eat hospital food that long, even if I could stay. He reasoned that just because I was being discharged from the hospital, it didn't mean that I could not come back and visit anytime I wanted.

He told me about a parent support group that was meeting on Tuesday night. The parents in the group had babies in the NICU, and they met twice a month to share their stories of success and frustration during their babies' hospital stay. Dr. Harding agreed to let me stay in the hospital until Wednesday morning if I agreed to attend the support group.

I begrudgingly agreed, but had already made up my mind I wasn't going to like it, and I wasn't going to participate in any discussion. When the time came Mike wheeled me down to the meeting place in a wheelchair. I was still in my hospital gown, and when we came into the room, it was obvious that we were the newest members of the group. Everyone else was nicely dressed in street clothes, and I instantly felt out of place as all eyes turned to me. I felt like I must have looked pathetic.

There were probably about 15 to 20 parents in the group. We arrived a few minutes late because I insisted on stopping by the NICU to get an update on Ryan. Members of the group were in the process of giving an update on the progress, or lack thereof, of their children.

I sat quietly and listened, intent on not participating. At the end of the meeting, Chris Frontino, the nurse who was facilitating the meeting, asked if there were any other questions or comments. It seemed that all eyes turned to me as I sat there quietly sobbing. I finally blurted out, *"HOW DID YOU LEAVE THE HOSPITAL WITHOUT YOUR BABY?!?"*

Every woman in that room identified with me at that moment. The meeting went on for at least another forty-five minutes as the women shared with me their feelings of having to go home alone, and how they overcame them. I learned that what I was feeling was normal. I learned that I would survive this first hurdle of having a premature baby.

## Leaving the Hospital...and Ryan

One young girl in the group named Shannon captivated me with the positive way that she shared about her son, Jimmy. She was bright and cheery, and had nothing but good things to say. Shannon came to me after the meeting and introduced herself. We went to the NICU together so we could show off our babies to one another. Jimmy was born on December 26, 1989. He weighed only one pound, ten ounces, and was born at about twenty-five weeks gestation. Shannon and I exchanged phone numbers before she left, and that was the beginning of a new friendship. *What I wouldn't give for that kind of faith,* I thought as Shannon left.

The next morning I had breakfast and put on the clothes that Mike had brought me the night before and cried at the thought of actually leaving Ryan. *What kind of mother am I to go off and abandon my son,* I thought. I walked down to the NICU for one last visit before the long ride home.

I stood at the window watching him sleep. He had white-blonde hair. He was the only "blondie" in the unit. He was already quite popular with all the nurses who would say to us, "Oh, you must be the parents of the towhead," when we came in to see him.

As I stood at the window, I heard: *"I said I would never give you more than you can handle."* I heard it with my ears and my heart. My memory took me back to a time a couple of years prior when I was walking through my living room with a towel over my head, drying my freshly washed hair. I heard, *"I will never give you more than you can handle"* as clearly as if someone was standing in the room with me. I took the towel from my face, and looked around the room. There was no one there. Mike was in the shower. We were both getting ready to go to work.

I had never experienced anything like that before. Later that day, as I was driving to my grandparents' house to have lunch with them, I heard a five-minute sermon on the radio. The topic was, *"How to know when God is speaking to you."* The example the minister gave was if someone had an enemy and he suddenly felt compelled to make amends, most likely it was God who spoke that into the mind. As human beings we don't just decide one day that we want to be friends with our enemies.

I recognized that it must have been God who spoke to me that morning. God was telling me that He will never give me more than I could handle. I got caught up in the fear that something bad was going to happen and I was going to have to handle it. I kept waiting. Nothing happened. I eventually forgot about the whole incident.

But on this day, standing at the window of the NICU, when I heard the words, *"I said 'I would never give you more than you could handle,'"* I knew that God was speaking to me. And I knew that he was going to see and me through this time. *"God, I promise to raise Ryan in a Christian home if you let him live,"* I prayed. Those were the first words I actually spoke to God about Ryan's situation. And I only spoke them after God first reached out to me. When I was dangling from my fraying rope of faith, God offered me a knot to hang on to. I grabbed on with everything I had.

# A New Routine

*The Lord is gracious and righteous; Our God is full of compassion. The Lord protects the simple hearted; when I was in great need, he saved me.*

*Psalm 116: 5-6*

Once home we had dozens of phone calls to make. Our answering machine was full of messages from well wishers and those who wanted updates on Ryan's condition. I spent a good portion of Wednesday afternoon on the phone trying to explain his prognosis and answer all the questions that people were asking. It was exhausting, and became quite burdensome over the next several days. Mike and I would come home late from the hospital every night, and leave early in the morning, so returning calls just didn't fit into the schedule.

That's when we came up with the idea to record *"The Ryan Report"* as the outgoing message on our answering machine. Every couple of days I would update the report, giving the status of his condition. After that, we came home to a lot of messages that were wishing us well, extending prayer support and thanking us for the update. We were relieved of the need to return phone calls. This system worked very well.

It was comforting to know that people we didn't even know were praying for Ryan and upholding Mike and me in prayer. It was hard for me to pray, and ask God for His will in Ryan's life. Because, in my heart, I only wanted God's will if it were His will for my baby to live and be healthy. But I knew that other people were praying for God's will for all of us, and that brought me great comfort.

It was an adjustment for us to get used to our new daily routine. Normally we would get up when the alarm went off, get ready for work, have breakfast together and head off to work. I was on maternity leave from work, but Mike had his work that he needed to do. To complicate matters, his office was being renovated, so he and all of his colleagues were moved to an empty court room in Downey where they all shared one phone line. Mike had just received a new assignment with the Los Angeles County Probation Department that nearly doubled his case load.

Dad loaned Mike a pager in the event we needed to reach him. It was to be used for emergencies only. Everyone in the courtroom was put on alert that if the phone rang, and it was me, they were to track Mike down immediately. He made a point of letting as many people as possible know his whereabouts. It got to the point that everyone in the office knew even when he went to the men's room.

I spent every day at the hospital with Ryan. Since I was not released by the doctor to drive right away, Mom would give me a ride to the hospital every morning, and Mike would come there after work. We would spend a couple of hours together as a family and leave around 6:00 p.m. Usually, we would stop for dinner on the way home.

I started getting used to the sights and sounds of the NICU. I learned that every time Ryan's monitor would ping, it meant that he was experiencing apnea-brady/cardia, or AB spells. The apnea occurred when he stopped breathing. Brady/cardia occurred when his heart rate dropped below normal due to the lack of oxygen. When he would forget to breathe, and his heart rate would drop, the machine would ping. This alerted the nurse, who would come over and stimulate Ryan by rubbing his back. He would then start to breathe again, which would bring his heart rate back up to normal and stop the pinging of the machine. The nurse would record how low his heart dropped and how soon Ryan started breathing again on his medical chart for his respiratory therapist, and reset the machine. This was an everyday occurrence at first. Some days it was an every hour occurrence, and sometimes several every hour occurrences.

When we met the neonatologist, Dr. Padilla, I knew that Ryan was in good hands. She was soft-spoken and seemed to be very knowledgeable. She was careful to explain everything that Ryan was experiencing, and she was very up front with us when we asked questions. She did not try to shield us from reality, but at the same time, she spoke in a positive, detailed manner that was easy for us to understand. She gave us hope.

Every day a nurse would poke Ryan's heel with a needle and take a blood sample to monitor his blood gases, a measurement of the amount of oxygen, carbon dioxide and acid in his blood. These measurements were needed to make adjustments in how much oxygen he should be receiving. He was receiving his nutrition by intravenous feeding. He was still on the Aminophyllin so that he would not sleep soundly and forget to breathe. He was being weaned off of the morphine that was given to calm his sensitive nervous system.

Within hours after Ryan was born, it was evident that he was in need of a blood transfusion. His body was not producing the red blood cells it needed. I requested that he receive blood from a family member, but at this point, there was not enough time to process the blood for his use.

Once the blood is drawn from a donor, there is a three-day process that it had to be put through, which included cleansing the blood and separating it into three components - white blood cells, red blood cells and platelets. As it would turn out, Ryan needed five separate blood transfusions during his hospital stay. During the other four transfusions he received blood from his grandma twice (my mom), his great aunt, Sharon (my mom's sister) and his grandpa (my dad).

On January 30, when Ryan was just nine days old, he reached up to the ventilator tube that was inserted into his mouth and gave it a pull. He pulled the tube out of his mouth and was breathing on his own for the first time. His nurse watched him do this and took a Polaroid picture to commemorate this occasion. She said that Ryan decided it was time to get rid of that tube.

He stayed off of the ventilator for a few days before it was evident that he would have to be re-intubated, which means they put him back on the ventilator. This was just one of many setbacks in Ryan's recovery that we would experience.

Mike and I would call the hospital every night before we went to bed and every morning after we got up. We tried to talk to the nurse who was in charge during that shift so she could tell us how he was doing instead of reading it off of a chart. We made it a point to call before shift changes. We recorded every call on a yellow lined tablet so we could chart Ryan's progress, or lack thereof. A typical record of the call went like this:

*1/24/90, 9:48 p.m. Valerie*
*Suctioning every three hours. Sleeping good. Will leave on back until morning. Is under billi lights for jaundice.*

## A New Routine

*2/1/90, 6:24 a.m. Sharon*
*Doing good. Had 2 AB spells. Feeding good. Slight temperature*
*Lost 20 grams, down to 830 (1 pound 13 ounces) Still in the normal range.*
*Very active.*

Ryan lost weight, like every baby does after birth. But when you don't have much to start with, every ounce makes a big difference. His lowest weight was at about one pound, eight ounces before he started gaining weight. A large weight gain was not necessarily a good thing. Usually it meant that the baby was experiencing pulmonary edema, or fluid retention in the lungs. This would start a series of administrations of Lasix to relieve the fluid, which would result in a large weight loss. Many times the weight loss was higher than the weight increase, and he would weigh less than when he started. This cycle went on for many weeks while Ryan's lungs were growing strong enough to do their job.

# Feeding Time

*Like newborn babies, crave pure spiritual milk, so that by it you may grow up In your salvation, now that you have tasted the Lord is good.*

                                                    1 Peter 2:2-3

I was encouraged by Ryan's doctor and every nurse in the unit to start pumping breast milk immediately after his birth. The milk would be placed in a freezer with Ryan's name and medical number on it for future use. This became a major challenge for me. My body was not ready to produce milk.

Within several days of Ryan's birth, Dr. Padilla determined that it was time to see if he could tolerate real food. For the first several weeks of feeding, he received his milk by the *gavage* method. This entailed placing a tube though Ryan's nose and down into his stomach. Once the tube was placed, it became a permanent feature until he could start sucking on a bottle. To insert and remove the tube during each feeding would be too traumatic for one so small.

Once the tube was in place, milk would be placed in a large syringe and hooked up to a machine that would slowly push the milk through the tube and into Ryan's stomach. His first feeding consisted of two CCs of milk. This is less than a teaspoon full. Then we would wait to see if his under-developed digestive system was going to tolerate the milk.

I continued to try to pump breast milk, and as time went on I became more and more frustrated to the point of tears. I would bring my three or four ounces in a Playtex bottle liner labeled with Ryan's name to the community freezer in NICU. The first time I did this, I was excited to get those few ounces. But when I opened that freezer and saw all those bottles filled to the top, I was feeling quite inadequate. It looked as though the Jerseymaid cows had just made a delivery, and my puny little bottles looked pathetic.

I received a lot of well meaning advice during those days: put a picture of Ryan in front of you when you pump, try lying down while you pump, drink a glass of wine before you pump, play soft music while you pump. But the best advice I received was from a nurse named Janie who said to me, "Why are you letting yourself get upset over this? Ryan is being fed. We have formula for him. He's not going to starve to death. You need to let this go and quit letting yourself get upset. Twenty years from now it's not going to matter whether he had your breast milk or our formula."

I felt like such a failure. I couldn't even feed my own child. I had arrived in the NICU in tears after trying to pump in the private room the hospital provided just for that purpose. Janie's words of wisdom allowed me to let myself off the hook. The next day I returned the rented breast pumping machine. Now more than, 20 years later, Janie's words have rung true.

# An Encounter with a Tall, Dark Stranger

*I am sending him to you for the express purpose that you may know our circumstances and that he may encourage your hearts.*
*Colossians 4:8*

We had many days of ups and downs while in the NICU. Our theme song became *"What a Difference a Day Makes."* We could go in there one day and Ryan would be progressing by leaps and bounds. Then, the next day, he would have a major setback. On one particular day he decided that he just didn't want to continue breathing. He had several AB spells before we arrived for a visit. After we arrived he went through an episode where every few seconds he would stop breathing. We were quickly ushered out of the NICU and the drapes were drawn to avoid prying eyes.

Ryan's nurse suggested that we go down to the cafeteria and get some coffee while his doctors tried to determine why, at this late stage in his progress, he would start experiencing these problems. We were terrified, but we took Pam's advice and went down to have some coffee.

When we returned to NICU it was shift changing time, so we had to wait a few more excruciating minutes before we could find out what was going on. Once the unit was reopened we went to Ryan's bedside and he seemed to be doing better. Doctors and nurses were puzzled because they had done nothing to correct the problem. It just seemed that he decided to return to a normal breathing pattern. Just as quickly as the problem started, it was resolved. Doctors never did figure out why this happened.

That night, before we left the NICU, we held hands over the Isolette and each held one of Ryan's little hands so we could pray together as a family. This became a routine that continued well into Ryan's teen years. Maybe not the holding hand part, but we prayed together as a family every night from that point on.

After leaving the NICU we made our usual stop by what we fondly referred to as the "fat farm" to look at the full term babies that were born that day. On this particular night there was an African-American family huddled around the window looking at a brand new baby. We stopped and chatted with them for a while. The new baby's father stood proud at about six feet-five inches tall. He asked where our baby was, and we explained that he was a preemie, weighing less than two-and-a-half pounds, and was in the NICU.

"I only weighed three pounds myself," stated this tall man. I crumbled into tears. "Can I give you hug?" I asked him. He took me in his arms and we hugged as other family members patted and encouraged me. They shook hands with Mike and promised to pray for Ryan as we parted ways. God knew that I needed to hear those words of encouragement on that particular night. He sent us an angel of encouragement, and I went home knowing that we were going to make it through this.

# Jimmy Takes a Turn for the Worse

*Even in laughter the heart may ache, and joy may end in grief.*
*Proverbs 14:13*

*O my Comforter in sorrow, my heart is faint within me.*
*Jeremiah 8:18*

Shannon and I ran into each other almost every day at the hospital. We shared one another's concerns and hopes for our sons. Shannon continued to be bright and cheery for her son, Jimmy. Even when Jimmy was having a bad day, Shannon showed him nothing but encouragement when she was with him.

On Sunday, February 4 when Mike and I walked into the NICU, we knew something was not right. There were bright lights and doctors and nurses surrounding Jimmy's isolette. The doctor inquired if anyone had been able to find Jimmy's mom. Someone said that they were still trying.

Mike and I were ushered out of the unit, as is customary when there is a baby in distress. No parents are allowed into a unit when there is a serious situation with a baby. Mike and I went home and prayed for little Jimmy… and our Ryan.

## Jimmy Takes a Turn for the Worse

On Monday we received a call from Shannon's mom that Jimmy did not make it. He got an infection called Necrotizing Enterocolitis (NEC), which is an infection of the bowel that causes the lining to swell or perforate. The belly becomes hard and distended, and when not treated soon enough, the bowel dies and the body becomes septic. NEC is one of the most difficult setbacks that can affect a baby in the NICU. We were devastated by the news. This was the first time since Ryan's birth that we had experienced death in the NICU.

Monday evening I called Shannon to see how I could help. She asked Mike and me to come and sit with her for a while. My heart sank at first. The loss that Shannon was experiencing hit too close to home. But Shannon was such a strong, positive person for me when I needed her. Now she needed me, and I couldn't let her down. When we left for the short six-mile drive to Shannon's house, it was dark, cold, windy and raining harder than I could remember it ever raining before. We sat with Shannon until the wee hours of the morning. We cried together as Shannon shared her memories of Jimmy's short life.

As we sat there grieving together, in the back of my mind, I kept thinking *this could be me pretty soon*. We came home around one in the morning, and cried some more. I relied a lot on Shannon's strength during our visits at the hospital. I knew that I was going to miss seeing her there. Now I would have to rely even more on my own faith that God was working out His purpose.

Shannon grieved the loss of Jimmy. But when the grieving was over she took that experience and turned it around. Just as the Bible says, that which the devil intends for evil, God will use for good. Shannon started nursing school. She can share her medical knowledge and personal experience with others in need. Shannon and her husband, Don, have two children now. But she still misses Jimmy, and speaking of him can still bring a tear to her eye.

After Ryan came home from the hospital, I felt guilty because he survived. Even today, I feel a little pang of guilt when I think about Jimmy. I wonder what Jimmy would have grown up to be. I wonder if he and Ryan would be best buddies. But it's comforting to know that Jimmy is rejoicing with the angels in heaven. And some day we will all see him again.

# Ryan is Moved

*Trust in the Lord with all your heart, and lean not on your own understanding.*

*Proverbs 3:5*

It is customary for the babies to be moved around within a unit for staffing purposes. Ryan was now a three-to-one baby, which meant that his nurse would be caring for at least two babies, and maybe three during her shift. When I went to see him on Tuesday following Jimmy's death, his isolette was not in its usual spot by the window. After spending the night with Shannon and grieving the loss of Jimmy, I was living on raw nerves and began to panic.

My first thought was that Ryan was moved back to unit 288 with the critical babies, and I made a mad-dash for that unit. Not seeing him there, I returned to his unit to seek him out.

He had been moved to the very spot where Jimmy's isolette had been. Irrationality moved in quickly as I demanded that Ryan be moved from that spot. I took the nurses by surprise with my anger and insistence that Ryan be moved. That was Jimmy's spot. I don't know if I was feeling a sense of disrespect because they were so quick to give Jimmy's spot to someone else, or if I didn't want Ryan there because of what happened to Jimmy. All I know is that all rational thinking had left me at that moment.

Once I could regain my composure and explain why it was that I wanted Ryan moved out of "Jimmy's place" they were quick to accommodate my request. I left the unit during the move and tried to regain my composure. I had a weak moment of faith, and resolved not to let that happen again.

It was my job to give Ryan his daily bath. I did this by putting warm water in a blue plastic bowl and giving him a sponge bath. He was not real happy with this procedure at first. As the days went by, he began to understand that it didn't hurt. I wasn't poking him with a needle or taking his temperature, or turning him over from front to back just when he got comfortable.

Ryan was eventually weaned off of the ventilator, but he required oxygen that was only two percent above room air for almost his entire stay in the hospital. Every time they would try to wean him from the two percent, he would have frequent AB spells.

Instead of the oxygen tubes in his nose, he had a round plastic oxygen hood over his head. It reminded me of a top to cake plate. There was a small area cut so it would fit over his shoulders. When my brother, Scott came to visit and saw Ryan's new oxygen hood he said, "Oh, Ryan under glass." We all had a good laugh over that. During times of high stress, having some comic relief really helped.

During Ryan's *"gavage"* feedings, the nurses would give him a pacifier that was made out of a rolled-up washcloth with a nipple taped to it. This was supposed to teach him to suck while he was feeding. The end result should have been for Ryan to put the sucking motion together with feeling satisfied in the tummy.

This may have been a good idea in principal, but it would take him several weeks after he was released from the hospital to stop holding his breath during a feeding. He just couldn't get that suck, swallow, breathe cycle down right.

# Holding Ryan for the First Time

*Let your father and mother be glad, and let her who gave you birth rejoice*

*Proverbs 23:25*

When Ryan was exactly three weeks old I got to hold him for the very first time. No words can describe what it felt like to finally have that baby in my arms. I also got to dress him for the first time. I bought a baby blue preemie-sized tee shirt for him to wear. It fit him like a dress. It was bad enough that the preemie-sized diapers came up to his nipples, now he had a tee shirt that came down to his ankles. But at least now he had clothes on.

It was quite a challenge to get him and all of his tubes and wires out of the isolette and into my waiting arms. During the time that he was out of his isolette his nurse continuously monitored his body temperature. We sat under a heat lamp. It lasted for only five minutes, but it felt like five seconds to me. After that first day Mike and I would trade off days. We each took our turn holding him for five minutes under a heat lamp until he could maintain his own body temperature.

The following Sunday Mike and I rode to the hospital with my mom and dad. We had already planned to let "Grandma" hold Ryan on that day. But to cover our surprise we jokingly argued with each other about who was going to hold him. When we arrived at the NICU we all donned our hospital gowns over our clothes and participated in the three-minute scrub routine so we could go into the unit.

I pulled a vacant chair over to Ryan's isolette and instructed my mom to sit down. The nurse came over and prepared Ryan for his excursion outside of his warm little world and placed him in my mom's arms. She was so overwhelmed with joy that she began to cry. We are not allowed to cry on the babies, so the nurse stood next to her and wiped her tears as she cherished the moment of holding her grandson for the very first time.

Soon Ryan was keeping his body temperature up without the need of a heat lamp. This is when we started a program called Kangaroo Care. Every day I would hold Ryan skin-to-skin on my chest. This was a relatively new therapy that encouraged bonding between parent and child, as well as helped the baby to develop quicker. Mike got into the action, too. Ryan got to the point where he could stay outside of his isolette longer and longer, so we would participate in Kangaroo Care therapy for longer periods of time.

We would laugh when Mike was the Kangaroo Care giver because Mike's chest hair tickled Ryan's nose and he would make the funniest faces. Nurse Pam came up with a quick solution and placed a *HandiWipe* under Ryan's head on Mike's chest. Something told me she had seen this before. She knew just what to do.

Now Kangaroo Care therapy is practiced worldwide. There are people who volunteer at neonatal intensive care units just to provide Kangaroo Care for babies whose parents are not capable of providing it. Many babies born into a NICU have drug addicted moms and soon become wards of the court. These babies need an opportunity to grow and develop, too.

# Ryan the Fighter

*Fight the good fight of the faith. Take hold of the eternal life to which you were called when you made your good confession in the presence of many witnesses.*

1 Timothy 6:12

Ryan was quite a fighter, and already we were starting to see a bit of personality in him. He did not like to be bothered when he was sleeping. He did not like the ventilator. And he hated the bright lights of the heat lamp. My Grandpa Black (Dad's dad) had emphysema. He was a fighter too. Grandpa was not well enough to go to the hospital and visit Ryan, so he sent him a gift. It was a small pair of boxing gloves that you might see hanging on someone's rearview mirror. They were attached together by a string, which was taped to the inside of Ryan's isolette. They were taped next to a sign that read, "I'm a mart tid." Everyone who saw the sign would ask us what it meant. It was a family saying that started when my brother, Scott, did something he was quite proud of when he was just a lad. When my mom pointed out his accomplishment he patted himself on the back by saying, "I'm a pretty mart tid." That translated into, "I'm a pretty smart kid." We made the sign for Ryan when he pulled his ventilator tube out for the first time. On the other side of the sign, it said, "Jesus Loves Me."

Grandpa Black fought his cancer and emphysema long enough to meet his little great-grandson. Ryan was released from the hospital less than a year before Grandpa went into the hospital to fight his last few days on this earth. Ryan still has those boxing gloves.

# Ryan, Can you Find Mommy?

*When he has brought out all his own, he goes ahead of them, and his sheep follow him because they know his voice. But they will never follow a strange; in fact, they will run away from him because they do not recognize a strager's voice.*
John 10:4-5

When Ryan was about eight weeks old he was put through a series of tests by his occupational therapist. I always thought it sounded funny for a newborn, without an occupation, to have an occupational therapist. Ryan had one of the best at Long Beach Memorial/Miller Children's Hospital.

After I arrived at the hospital I dressed Ryan in a LBM/MCH long-sleeved infant tee shirt. I had to triple roll the sleeves to find his hands. Once dressed the OT place Ryan on a blanket-covered counter and performed a series of tests. She flashed a light in his eyes to see how he responded. She used a variety of rattles to see how he responded to various sounds. The final test came when she held him up in her arms away from her body and had me stand at the same distance away from him on the other side. She had me start calling his name, while she would call his name and ask him to find Mommy. I would say, "Ryan, look at Mommy," and she would say, "Ryan, can you find

Mommy?" Within a minute Ryan was turning his head and trying to find me. He recognized my voice and could distinguish it from a less familiar voice.

I can't tell you what joy I felt in my heart to see my little boy looking for me. The OT placed him in my arms and I hugged and kissed him while trying not to soak him with my tears of pride and joy. The OT had the whole thing taped on a VHS tape and gave me a copy of the tape. The sound didn't work, but when I watch that tape today, I can recall the sounds and the joy of the day.

# Taking a Day to Myself

*Come to me, all you who are weary and burdened, and I will give you rest.*
*Matthew 11:28*

After spending a solid two months of making that twenty-six-mile trip to the hospital every single day, I was beginning to tire. Ryan's nurses ganged up on me one day and convinced me that I needed to take a day to myself. It took a lot of convincing because I felt that I needed to be with my little guy every day. I felt that he was always waiting for me to come and visit him and if I didn't show up I would let him down somehow. Finally, they were able to convince me that Ryan would survive without me for one day. I made an appointment to get a permanent. It was a Wednesday.

Mike and I had been going to Papillon Coufieur in La Mirada since before we were married. Two of Mike's sisters also went there, and when we were there it was like old home night. We knew all the hair dressers, and they all knew about Ryan. When I arrived for my appointment everyone wanted to know how things were going and they wanted to see pictures.

After all the hoopla settled down and my hairdresser, Joseph, started working on my hair I became anxious. I realized that I was away from my phone. I had given Ryan's nurse the phone number of the beauty shop, but

I started thinking about what would happen if she forgot where I would be. What if something happened and they couldn't find me? Have you ever played the "what if" game? That is a game I was very good at.

By the time Joseph had half of my head rolled in perm rods, I was panic stricken. By the time he got me under the hair dryer I was in tears. I didn't even let him dry or style my hair. As soon as I got to a point that I could leave the shop I headed home so I could call in and check on Ryan. The next day I went into the hospital with a new hairdo. Ryan's nurses congratulated me on giving myself a day off. I chastised them and told them that I would never miss a day of visiting my son. It wasn't a day of rest for me. It was one of the longest days of my life. I understand why the nurses did what they did. I'm sure they try to do the same with all the moms who suffer from NICU fatigue after a while. But that was the last day that I missed a visit with Ryan. I never missed another day until the day he came home.

As time went on everyone wanted to throw Ryan a baby shower. I think it was people's way of saying, "We believe Ryan's going to make it. He's going to be okay." We attended five baby showers before he came home. Our most memorable one was held at Scotty's Restaurant. As I said before, it was one of our favorite places to eat. We frequented Scotty's during Ryan's hospital stay. All of the waitresses and regular customers knew about Ryan and would always ask how he was doing.

Debbie Christle, the wife of Scotty's owner, Scott, closed down the restaurant on a Sunday afternoon for a private baby shower. All the waitresses came, and many of the regular customers were there. The restaurant was decorated with baby streamers that were left up for several days following the shower.

Debbie was one of my drivers, too, who would take me to the hospital and stay with me for a couple of hours. She was a great friend during a difficult time. Right after Ryan's birth Debbie gave me a tan and white teddy bear, similar to one of the Care Bears of cartoon fame. I slept with that teddy bear every night that Ryan was in the hospital. I still have it.

My friends that I worked with at Fedco Department Store's main office in Santa Fe Springs, California, threw me a shower also. I hadn't worked with them in almost a year, but they were great friends and wanted to share in our joy. It served as a mini reunion as we reminisced about my days at Fedco, working as a clerk in the human relations and training departments. Ryan's aunties on his dad's side of the family hosted a shower. We showed videos of Ryan during the shower so those who had not been able to visit could see him. There were also two family showers on my side of the family, one by the Blacks and one by the Bickerstaffs. By the time he did come home we had acquired so many gifts that we barely had room in our little 1200 square foot home for the baby.

We couldn't believe that two months had passed since Ryan's birth, but at the same time, it seemed like an eternity. One of his nurses asked if we had bought a crib yet. Mike and I looked at each other, realizing we hadn't thought that far. We hadn't even thought of the day that Ryan would come home. Where would he sleep? The nurse politely admonished us and explained how important it was that he had the comfort of his own bed, and not sleep in ours. So the hunt was on for the perfect crib. We settled on a solid oak crib we found at a place in Brea called The Baby Barn. We also ordered a wall hanging of his name in primary colors that was made out of puffy letters stuffed with batting. It was about two feet high and four feet wide. We had to order the crib to be custom-made, which would take a while.

We figured when we ordered it that we had plenty of time, since no one had even muttered a word about Ryan coming home anytime soon.

# Bottle Feeding – Suck, Swallow, **Breathe**

*The Spirit of God has made me, and the breath of the Almighty gives me life.*

*Job 33:4*

The day finally came when it was time for Ryan to start receiving his milk from a real bottle instead of a tube through his nose. What a great day it was to get rid of that tube. He was a slow learner when it came to the rhythm of eating. He had it all wrong. A baby that is born full term learns the sucking and swallowing techniques in the womb. They suck their thumbs and swallow fluid before they are born. All they have to do is incorporate the breathing technique once they are born.

Preemies have to learn the process backwards. It's imperative that they learn to breathe as soon as possible after they are born. After several weeks they are then introduced to the suck and swallow steps of eating. The rhythm of eating is suck, swallow, breathe, suck, swallow, breathe and so on, until they are done eating.

Ryan didn't get this rhythm down at first. In fact, it wasn't until after he came home that he figured out how to do this. A typical feeding session went more like this: suck, swallow, suck, swallow, suck, swallow, start turning blue, remove bottle, pant, pant, pant. He couldn't seem to get the message that he somehow had to incorporate breathing in with eating.

The bottles that we used in the hospital were small cylinders that held two ounces of formula or breast milk. If Ryan got down one ounce during a feeding we were jumping for joy. At one point he got so tired during his feedings that he wasn't getting enough nutrition. It was then that Dr. Padilla decided to put the *gavage* tube back in to give Ryan a break. This was just one of many steps backwards that we took during our stay. As it turned out he was getting weaker because it was time for another blood transfusion. We could always tell when it was time for a transfusion because he would start looking dusky and pale.

# Growing in Grace and Size

*But grow in the grace and knowledge of our Lord and Savior*
*Jesus Christ. To him be the glory now and forever! Amen*
                                                *2 Peter 3:18*

Finally the time came when Ryan was moved up to what was called the growing room. This is the last step a baby takes before going home. Babies in the growing room were healthy, eating and breathing on their own, and only needed to gain weight before they could go home. The move into the growing room was a huge step for a baby. It was a big step for parents, too. We had to leave all the nurses that we spent several weeks getting to know and move into a room where we weren't familiar with any of the staff or procedures. Babies in this room didn't need to be monitored as closely as before.

Fortunately, Ryan's nurse Mary once worked in the unit that he just moved out of, so we were familiar with her. Mary was a grandmotherly African-American woman with a smile as big as Texas. She had an infectious laugh that just lit up the room. We could tell that she really enjoyed her job. We were so glad that she would be our nurse for the duration of his stay.

Ryan was now in an open crib. He no longer needed oxygen and he was eating fairly well. It was time to really start talking about going home. As excited as I was to finally get him home, I also started getting very nervous.

Finally, on March 21, Dr. Padilla approached us with a tentative date. Our baby could possibly come home as early as Sunday, April 1. Joy and panic hit me at the same time. He would come home on medication, which needed to be administered around the clock, every three hours. He would be tested to see if he needed an apnea monitor at home. There were several last-minute tests to be conducted. And he was going to need one more blood transfusion before he was released.

I started to panic when I realized we would be on our own. There would be no nurses around to make sure Ryan was okay. I would have to trust my motherly instincts. I didn't know if I was up to this. And the crib hadn't arrived yet. Where was this baby going to sleep?

We were preparing to pick up Ryan that Sunday morning when we got a call from the hospital. The nurse told us that he was running a slight temperature, which could indicate that he had an infection somewhere. The doctor on duty decided to postpone the homecoming so they could keep an eye on him. If everything went well over the next couple of days, perhaps Ryan could come home on Wednesday, April 8. I felt disappointment and relief.

By Tuesday Ryan's fever was gone and he showed no sign of infection so we were given the go ahead to take him home the next day. When I woke up on Wednesday morning I called the hospital just to make sure we were still on schedule. The nurse informed me that Ryan had shown an abnormal weight gain overnight, and could be experiencing a bout of pulmonary edema. Again, our homecoming was postponed. I was beginning to think that Ryan should stay in the hospital for another few weeks. Mike could sense my growing anxiety. He suggested we take some time to ourselves and visit the duck park. We realized that once our little guy made it home we would be spending a lot of time there. So off to the park we went.

We stopped at the bread store and bought our usual ten loaves for a dollar. It was spring time and there were a lot of mother ducks with their little ducklings. It was my favorite time of the year to feed the ducks. Along with the mallards and white pekin ducks, there were American coots. Coots are black with a white beak, greenish-yellow legs and webbed feet. While the other ducks had their ducklings out swimming in the open, the coots kept their young safely hidden in the reeds along the shore.

I was enjoying feeding the ducklings. It was good to get away from my worries for little while. Mike was about ten feet away from me feeding the coots along the reeds. He called me over to look at something. "I want you to watch this mama coot when I toss a piece of bread to her," he said. I watched, not sure what I was supposed to see.

Mike tossed her a piece of bread and she soaked it in the water. She carried it in her beak over to the edge of the reeds. Once she got to the edge she put the bread down in the water and squawked. Several ducklings came to the edge and she fed them, mouth-to-mouth, one at a time, with the bread.

"If God gave this bird enough common sense to know how to take care of her young, don't you think he has given you what you need to know how to take care of Ryan?" he said. I started crying. God used a coot to let me know that he believes in me and my parenting capabilities. I left the park that day with a new attitude. I was now more excited than anxious about Ryan's homecoming.

Sunday, April 8, was here. We would finally be bringing our son home. We got up early and called the hospital to see how Ryan's night was. Again, he started to run a fever in the night and his doctors were not ready to let him come home. We casually got dressed and went out to breakfast on our way to the hospital to visit him.

While we were at the hospital we met with Dr. Padilla to go over everything we needed to know before Ryan came home. She said that she was shooting for April 11 as the next target date to release him.

The NICU was short on babies, which is always a real good thing. We have been there when it was busting at the seams and every unit was filled. But during this time there was one unit that was completely empty. Dr. Padilla suggested that Mike and I come early Tuesday morning and spend the entire day at the hospital with Ryan. We would be his caregivers, administering all of his medications and feedings. It was determined that Ryan would be on an apnea monitor at home, and Dr. Padilla wanted us to be comfortable working with the machine. She reserved the empty unit for us to stay in all day with Ryan. It would be just the three of us.

We left the hospital early enough to attend the evening service at our church. With Ryan in the hospital our church attendance had been rather lacking. It was nice to be back. We requested prayer for Ryan, asking that he would be able to come home on Wednesday, as planned.

We had a guest speaker that night. He talked about the need to ask Jesus into our hearts and to live a life worthy of calling Jesus our Lord and Savior. He asked anyone who has not asked Jesus into his or her heart if they would like to come up to the front of the church and pray with someone. I leaned over and whispered in Mike's ear, "Have you ever committed your life to Christ?" I knew he believed in Christ. But I felt that God was really speaking to his heart that night.

"I promised God that if he let Ryan live, I would raise him in a Christian home," I told Mike. "I can't do that without you. Maybe God is waiting for you to make that commitment before Ryan comes home."

Mike left the pew and walked up to the front of the church. I followed him for support. That night Mike gave his life to Christ. Ryan wasn't even three months old and he had an impact on his daddy's life. I knew Ryan would be coming home on Wednesday.

On Tuesday, April 10, we went to spend our day at the hospital. Ryan was moved into the vacant unit and all the curtains were drawn so we didn't feel like everyone was watching us. Ryan was hooked up to the same type of apnea monitor we would be using at home and we were given last minute instructions on medications and feedings. Then we were on our own.

It was a very long day. Mary would come in and check on us from time to time. We took a picnic lunch so we wouldn't have to leave to get something to eat. The day was fairly uneventful. Ryan's apnea monitor went off occasionally when he stretched. But he never had any AB spells.

We left the hospital Tuesday night sure that we would be taking Ryan home the next morning. We went home and got the last good night's sleep without interruptions that we would get for several weeks.

Wednesday morning we got up, got dressed and called the hospital to see if Ryan was going to get to come home. We knew this was the day. Ryan was ready. We were ready. Mom came with us to the hospital for moral support and to video tape the joyous occasion.

We knew Mary wouldn't be there because it was her day off. We said our goodbyes to her on Tuesday. I was really going to miss her. When we got to the hospital I dressed Ryan in the outfit I had picked out for the homecoming. He was taken out for his hospital pictures while his doctor went over all of the prescriptions and we signed the release forms. Finally, it was time to leave. Eighty days after I delivered a two-pound, six-ounce baby boy, Ryan left the only "home" he knew and came home with his mom and dad, weighing just over four pounds. God had carried us through just like he promised.

*Presenting*
*Ryan Michael Tommer*

*God's Little Miracle*

*On January, 21, 1990, I was born,*
*a bundle so small.*
*At 2 pounds, 6 ounces, I surprised them all.*

*At Long Beach Memorial*
*I had a shaky start.*
*I had to work hard to strengthen*
*my lungs and my heart.*

*Mommy and Daddy were there with me*
*each day and some nights,*
*and each day I grew stronger.*
*Boy, I put up a fight.*

*Nurse Pam was beside me*
*with special love and care,*
*and with God watching over,*
*there was much love to share.*

*I arrived home on April 11th*
*and I'm learning from day and night.*
*I'm trying to be in charge,*
*but now, Mom and Dad put up a fight.*

*Now we are all working hard*
*on our daily routine,*
*and I'm now the resident of*
*the finest nursery you've seen.*

*Written by Margie Black*
*For Ryan's birth announcement*

*Part 2*

# FAITH BEYOND EIGHTY DAYS

The homecoming was much anticipated. Once Ryan was home it took a few weeks to get used to the new normal. Ryan's first bed was a bassinette that had been handed down and used by his two cousins, Denise and Kim. With each new baby, Mike's Aunt Zoe would replace the bedding, as well as the taffeta and lace around the outside of the bed. This time she adorned it with beautiful blue ribbon. Ryan was the first boy born in his generation, and the first boy in his immediate family since Mike was born. He was also the first grandbaby for my mom and dad. By now, you can probably imagine just how excited everyone was to have this little guy finally home.

Our normal schedule included administering medication every three hours around the clock. He came home on Theofolin, Reglan, a multivitamin and vitamin D drops. The Theofolin was an oral version of what he received in his IV at the hospital. Essentially, it was caffeine. It kept him from falling into a deep sleep. The Reglan was given to help with acid reflux and the constant projectile vomiting that became part of life for the next several months. The Vitamin D helped to prevent rickets.

Ryan's medications would be administered in about 10ccs of formula before his feedings. He still had not mastered the suck-swallow-breathe sequence that he needed for a smooth eating experience. A typical day started at 3:00 a.m. with his first feeding. He was then wakened and fed every three hours, with his last feeding in a 24-hour period at midnight.

With this routine it may sound like Ryan was eating a lot, but if we got two ounces of formula down him in one feeding we were happy. He spent most of his days sleeping and growing. I spent most of my days watching him sleep. We set alarms for every three hours on the half hour so we could prepare Ryan's medications and bottles.

We were so structured at the hospital that it was very hard for us to relax. We kept a chart on the kitchen wall to show at what time Ryan would get his medications. One medication was administered every three hours, one every six hours, one every 12 hours and two every 24 hours. It took absolute concentration when administering his medication to make sure we gave the right one at the right time.

We also charted his bowel movements and when his diaper was changed. He was very constipated due to all of the medication, so this became a problem. We were so exhausted. It was easy to lose track of time between feedings.

We institutionalized our home. That was the only way we knew how to operate. When visitors came over they were escorted to the bathroom for the three-minute scrubbing of the hands. This was protocol before entering the NICU and we continued it once we got home.

For the first several days Mike and I would get up together for each feeding. As the nights wore on it was obvious that Mike needed some solid sleep because he still had to go to work every day. Eventually I felt comfortable enough to take care of Ryan by myself. I also learned to take advantage of power naps between feedings during the day. In the first few weeks at home Ryan slept most of the time. I would have to wake him up to feed him.

Working around the apnea monitor became a pain. The leads would come off and the monitor would ping. The wires would tangle. When we moved from room to room, we would have to move the monitor and make sure there was an accessible electrical outlet. Looking back, I realize the only time he needed to be on the monitor was when he was sleeping. That was the only time he would stop breathing when he was in the hospital. Being the new and slightly paranoid parents that we were, we kept him hooked up to that thing 24/7, except at bath time.

We did start taking him off the monitor at feeding times because his tendency to hold his breath during feedings caused it to go off continuously and unnecessarily. Since we were right there with him, and knew what to expect we didn't need a machine to tell us what was going on. Ryan struggled with that suck, swallow, breathe sequence for at least another month before he finally got the hang of it.

Our first dinner at home as a family was Chinese food brought to us by Mike's sister, Dee Dee. It was nice to be home and know we weren't going to be making that long trip back to the hospital. While we were enjoying our dinner Ryan's monitor went off for the first time. We all jumped up from the table to see what was going on. One of the leads had come off of Ryan's chest. While we all stood around breathing a sigh of relief Ryan quietly slept through the whole episode.

The Sunday following Ryan's homecoming was Easter. Mom and Dad came over for lunch. We took pictures of Ryan for his birth announcement, which was printed at Mom and Dad's print shop, with a poem written by Mom.

After a week of being housebound with Ryan I thought I was ready to get out. Because of the difficult feeding times, no one besides Mike wanted to tackle feeding time. Mom and Dad offered to come over and stay with Ryan while Mike and I went out to dinner. We decided to go to our old dig, Scotty's. We had to go between feedings, so it was just a quick dinner out.

I really was looking forward to getting out until it was actually time to walk out the door. After running down an unnecessary list of "what ifs" and "watch fors" we headed out. I cried all the way to the restaurant. When we pulled into the parking lot I opened the door almost before Mike got the car parked, raced into the restaurant, past the cash register and to the phone hanging on the wall next to where the waitresses picked up their hot food.

I called to make sure that in the twenty-minute drive to the restaurant everything had gone okay and to give Mom the phone number to the restaurant. Once I was reassured that nothing terrible had happened in the last twenty minutes I settled down and was ready to eat. It was like being at a reunion. We had missed the staff and all the other patrons. For a few minutes I felt like life was normal for the first time in three months.

As time went by we settled into our new normal. Things were moving right along. Ryan got much better at eating and was starting to gain weight. His special-order, solid oak crib was finally delivered and we got him settled into his own bedroom. Mike was back to a normal schedule at work, and I learned that I could function on a lot less sleep than I was used to. It's amazing what the body can do when it needs to.

On one very hot June night we were awakened by the shrill beeps of Ryan's apnea monitor. Mike and I both flew out of bed and ran for what seemed like an eternity down our fifteen-foot-long hallway. Ryan had stopped breathing and we had to get to him. This was the first emergency since Ryan had come home.

We flipped on the light to find Ryan sound asleep but breathing normally. Because it was such a hot and humid night one of the leads that attached to Ryan's chest had simply fallen off. That was the only time that Ryan's monitor went off in the darkness of the night. After we were assured that Ryan was okay Mike and I were wide awake. Unable to sleep, we turned on the coffee and broke out the Entenmann's coffee cake.

After Ryan had been home three months his pediatrician said that it was time for him to come off of the apnea monitor. He suggested that we turn in the monitor to the home health company that had been supplying it. Mike and I asked him what determines that a baby no longer needs to be monitored. Since he couldn't really give us a good answer we suggested that they perform a beat-to-beat or pneumagram before we take the monitor away. This is what determined that he needed the monitor to begin with.

After much discussion (or I should say debate) with the doctor we left the appointment with the understanding that we would keep the monitor until we could come to terms with this issue. A couple of weeks later the doctor called to let us know that he ordered the test.

A representative showed up from the home health care company and set Ryan up for the twelve-hour test. A week later we were informed that Ryan passed the test and we were finally rid of that machine that had been an extension of him since he came home from the hospital. By that time he had been weaned off of his medications.

The first night Ryan slept without his monitor I tried to sleep in the rocking chair in his room. I periodically shined a small light on him to make sure that he was breathing. I no longer had a machine to alert me to any breathing problems. That was a very long first machine-free night. But I eventually got used to not having the monitor as a back-up system and we were all sleeping through the night.

From that point on Ryan was just a baby like every other baby. Of course, to us he was special. But without the monitor and other tell-tale signs of his premature birth, he didn't draw the attention he used to draw when we were out and about.

Ryan turned out to be a very atypical preemie. When we left the hospital we were told that the typical things we could look for were a lot of allergy and asthma-related problems due to the prematurity of his lungs at birth, but he rarely ever got sick. He experienced his first and only severe asthma attack when he was six years old. It required a trip to the emergency room at five in the morning. His doctor later put him on a maintenance asthma medication, which he took for several years. He hasn't had a problem since.

We were told that Ryan would probably be developmentally slow. We noticed this at first, but he eventually made up for it. When he was a baby he would not hold his bottle. We would place his hands around it as he we held him and fed him. This was to try to teach him the center-line of gravity. Later on I could set that bottle down on the floor in front of him and he would just cry. He wouldn't reach out and grab it. Eventually he realized the freedom of holding his own bottle and not having to rely on someone to feed him.

Ryan was not walking by his first birthday, and hadn't learned to crawl. However, he was rolling everywhere. Matter of fact, he walked before he crawled. His pediatrician wanted him to learn to crawl, so when Ryan would start to walk, we would put him on his hands and knees and crawl around on the floor to demonstrate. He just looked at us like we were crazy. Why crawl when walking is so much more practical? We would put our couch cushions on the floor and crawl over them to make a game. Eventually Ryan caught on and the three of us were crawling all over the house together.

Time went on and he grew. I loved being a stay-at-home mom and took Ryan to mommy and me classes, the library, anyplace where he would be with kids his own age so he would learn from them. Ryan qualified for out-patient occupational therapy. Once a month we would take him to a center where someone would work with him on coordination. The therapist would have him put raisins in a small bottle to improve his fine motor skills. She would sit him on a three-by-three-foot platform and suspend it from the ceiling. As he played with toys they would gently swing it so Ryan would learn to balance himself. After six months he graduated from the program. He was no longer considered a child with needs.

When Ryan was about two-and-a-half years old Mike said it was time to think about having another baby. I was a bit hesitant. I had been volunteering at Whittier Pregnancy Care Center, a life-affirming crisis pregnancy center. There was an adoption attorney serving on the board at the time, and I had entertained the idea of adopting a baby.

When Mike brought up the idea of me getting pregnant again over dinner one night, my first thought was I can't do that again. How could I have a baby in the hospital and a toddler at home? I was assuming that another pregnancy would result in another premature delivery. And besides, the doctor who delivered Ryan discouraged me from getting pregnant again.

I asked Mike to give me a month to pray about having another baby. I knew I could not go into pregnancy with fear. I had to be sure it was the right thing to do. I prayed and at the end of the month I believed that God wanted us to have another baby. I put aside the idea of adopting and I got pregnant immediately, which surprised me because it took two years to get pregnant with Ryan.

During that month of prayer I visited a doctor with Kaiser Permanente who specialized in high-risk pregnancy. I told him of my experience with Ryan and that the doctor who delivered him suggested that I not have another baby. Dr. Grove's response was that he would work with me, and he would not discourage someone from having a baby based on one premature delivery.

During my pregnancy I saw Dr. Grove every two weeks and received an ultrasound at four months and another one at about five-and-a-half months. Things were going well. Dr. Grove was very positive and encouraging, and I was not worried. I knew this was a God thing, because I am a worrier by nature. But I felt peace.

At about twenty-five weeks I started experiencing cramps, similar to those that I experienced when Ryan was born. I called my doctor and he suggested I go into labor and delivery just to be monitored. I took Ryan to Moms, called Mike and told him I was just going in for some extra peace of mind and headed for the hospital.

Once there it was confirmed that I was having contractions and I was going to be admitted. I did not expect this at all. I was totally blindsided. I knew I had a bladder infection and told the nurses that I did. They said they tested me for that, and it came up negative. I was devastated. The doctor on call told me the baby probably weighed about one-and-a-half pounds and probably would not survive if they couldn't stop the contractions.

I was put on the slo-mag to stop the contractions. All I could think was, "God, why did you let me get pregnant if this was going to happen again?" As I lie alone in my little room that was big enough for one bed, in the dark, I cried.

Dr. Grove came to see me within two hours after I was admitted. Crying, I told him that I felt that I a bladder infection, but that the nurses wouldn't listen to me. It felt the same way as with Ryan, but I'd never had a bladder infection before so I didn't know that I had one. I spewed out all of this in rapid succession, as if I had to give him as much information as possible so he could help me.

Dr. Grove held up one finger and said, "Hold that thought. I'll be back in thirty minutes." When he returned he held in his arms a medical book that looked to be about five inches thick, open to a specific page. He told me there is a bladder infection that some women get when they are pregnant. As the baby grows it pushes on the bladder in a way that prevents the bladder from emptying completely. This causes bacteria to form in the bladder. He went on to say that the only way to know for sure if this type of infection has occurred is to do a seventy-two-hour culture of the urine. Since we didn't have seventy-two hours to wait for test results, he suggested that he start treating me for this type of bladder infection. If this was in fact the problem, I should respond to treatment within a couple of hours. Dr. Grove had the nurse start the IV drip. By the end of the day I was feeling great, the contractions had stopped, and I was released to go home. Seventy-two hours later, it was confirmed. Dr. Grove had solved the mystery.

I was on an antibiotic for the rest of my pregnancy and I gave birth do a beautiful six-pound, two-ounce baby girl. Samantha Nicole Tommer was born three weeks premature, but healthy and able to leave the hospital the same day I did. I thought it interesting that her weight was the opposite of Ryan's two pounds and six ounces.

I realized through my preterm contractions that God allowed me to see why Ryan was born early. I had spent a lot of time since his birth blaming myself, thinking I had done something to cause his premature birth. But it wasn't my fault. To know that was very freeing to me and gave me the ability to forgive myself for something I thought I had done.

Even though we had at least two ultrasounds during my pregnancy with Samantha, the technician could never tell the sex of the baby. She was quite modest. She was delivered by Cesarean section. When the doctor announced that it was a girl, Mike was dancing around the delivery room saying, "Praise God, Praise God." He caught me and the hospital staff off guard. Everyone got pretty quiet. Everyone, except Samantha, that is. She was lying on a very uncomfortable table waiting to be cleaned up and weighed. She was screaming at the top of her lungs. I could see her lying there, crying and I couldn't do anything for her. Mike walked over to her and said, "Oh, Precious." Samantha turned her head and looked at him with wide eyes as if to day, "Daddy?" She quieted down and there was no more crying. The nickname "Precious" stuck and at 19 years old, that's what her daddy still calls her.

Since Samantha came a week before my scheduled Cesarean section, Dr. Grove did not deliver her. As I was getting into the wheel chair to go home he hurried into my room to congratulate me. During our brief conversation he pointed to his head and mentioned the number of gray hairs my pregnancy had added to his head. He suggested that I not have any more babies. We laughed about that as I reminded him of his comment when we first met about how he would not discourage a woman from getting pregnant. We said our goodbyes and off we went with our new baby daughter. Dr. Grove continued to be my doctor for many years.

Ryan was three-and-half years old when Sam was born. He started preschool just a few weeks before she was born, and he loved it. The first day I dropped him off he waved good-bye and went right in. I cried all the way home. He didn't cry until I went to pick him up. He didn't want to come home. That didn't do much for my ego, but Ryan was where he needed to be, and he was learning. That was what was important.

Whatever Ryan lacked in physical coordination he more than made up for in mental ability. As he grew it became quite evident that he had a near photographic memory. One time, while at Denny's Restaurant with Mom and Dad, we discovered just how good that memory was. The restaurant had a kids' promotion in which they handed out round cards in a plastic container to the kids. Each card had a picture of one of the planets on it.

We gave Ryan the cards and he passed one out to each of us. A couple of us got one extra. He then collected the cards and put them back in the box. Soon we noticed that Ryan was studying the cards. He then passed them out again, giving each of us the very card(s) that he gave us the first time. When we realized what he was doing we started trading our cards among each other. We wanted to see if it was coincidence that he gave us our original cards. After we had shuffled our cards around between the four of us we gave them back to Ryan, who immediately reissued them in the original order he had first dealt them. Several days later I pulled out the planet cards. As I held up each card Ryan would tell who it was originally assigned to. I couldn't believe he had such a memory. But that was to be only the beginning.

Since Ryan was a tiny baby Mike would come home from work and read to him. As he got older they would read a book and share a Granny Smith apple. It soon became apparent that Ryan was doing much more than looking at the pictures.

Before Ryan was born, when I was working at Fedco, I would visit my grandparents weekly for lunch. This became a routine after Ryan was older and off of all his medications. Once a week we would take a ride to Grandma and Grandpa Bickerstaff's house for lunch. When Ryan was four we were taking one of our weekly trips. I was stopped at a signal when Ryan said, "Mom, does that sign say, 'Celebrate the moments of your life'?" I looked over at the billboard and saw an advertisement for International House Coffees. He read the sign!

Ryan was always thinking and analyzing everything. One morning while we were on our way to Bible study, he was very quiet. I knew he was unpacking something in his head. He would go to a pre-school group called C.O.W. Club (Children of the Word Club) while I attended a woman's Bible study. I would drop him off at the south campus of the church, then Sam and I would go up to north campus, where I would drop her off at the nursery.

On our way there Ryan developed the hiccups. As I pulled into the parking stall Ryan said, "Mom?" "Yes, Ryan." I replied. "If Jesus lives in my heart, then when I have the hiccups he will go up and down, and up and down, and bump his little head." How was I going to explain that to a four-year-old? I was running late for my study so I said, "Well, why don't we go in and talk with Miss Shelly about this," as I stifled a laugh. Ryan was always amusing us with his ponderings.

When he started Kindergarten it didn't take long for his teacher, Mrs. Palmer, to realize that he could read. One afternoon she asked if she could keep him after school and test his reading level. When I picked him up an hour later I asked her how he did. She said that he read up to eighth-grade level and probably could have gone higher, but that was the highest level of book she had available.

Ryan had missed the Kindergarten Roundup the school held each year to test children to see if they were ready for school. That was probably a blessing because, though Ryan could read, he was very reluctant to use a pencil. Most of the school's testing was scored on how well a child could write. Ryan would probably have been denied admittance based on his lack of writing skills.

On his sixth birthday Ryan received a game called "Elefun." My dad handed him the instructions and told him to read them to him as he assembled the game. Ryan started reading the directions in perfect Spanish. We all laughed as Dad told him to turn the instructions over and read the English side. As he read, Dad assembled the game.

Ryan was like a sponge. He loved to learn. School was his favorite place. He also loved to play games. One of his favorites was Trivial Pursuit. The problem was that he had a hard time finding people to play with him because he knew most of the answers. When he wasn't at school or playing games he was absorbing the History Channel or the National Geographic Channel.

When Ryan was twelve he got the board game "Cranium" for his birthday. It was a difficult, multifaceted game that no one else in the family liked to play. I would sit for what seemed like hours and read the cards to him. He answered most of the questions on them. I thought I finally found one that would stump him when I asked him what type of art Paul Signac and Georges Seurat developed in 1886. Ryan's response was, "Oh, that's easy. Pointillism." I turned the card over and it said, "Pointillism." "How did you know that?" I asked. He explained that he had learned that in the third grade from a teacher who taught an art class once a week.

"Why do you remember that after all these years?" I asked. "I don't know. I have a hard time forgetting things," he told me. Oh, to have that problem. To this day Ryan is the family go-to answer man. The only difference now is he's got his I-Phone to help him find the answers.

He is well on his way to finishing his bachelor's degree in music education. He is a history buff, especially the Civil War and Nazi Germany. During a family vacation to Gettysburg Ryan was our tour guide. He had just taken the same trip with his eight grade class, so he was stuffed full of historical information. In fact he had so much information that he turned a three-hour self-guided tour into six hours.

Ryan is an outstanding trumpet player and plans to teach high school band after he gets his degree in music education. He started trumpet lessons in the sixth grade. I remember the day he came home from school to find the rented trumpet I had picked up from the music store. I was in the kitchen when I heard this horrible noise coming from the living room. "Who let the elephant in the house?" I yelled from the kitchen. Ryan has been disciplined and diligent in his learning. He even received private lessons from DJ Barraclough, a member of the Dallas Brass. He has come a long way from that first elephant-sounding note.

As you can tell, I'm one proud momma. Thank you for allowing me to tell my story of how a two-pound, six-ounce premature baby helped me to grow in my faith in God as he grew in size and stature.

Though I have come to the end of my book, this is by far not the end of the story. Ryan is in the prime of his life. At twenty-three years old he has a lifetime of experience ahead of him. I forget that he started out on that January day in 1990 as a two-pound, six-ounce tiny baby fighting for every breath he took. But I never stop thanking God for the precious life he gave us. Through that little life we have learned that God is in control of every situation, and we must have faith that God will see us through the small things and the big things in life.

# Photo Gallery

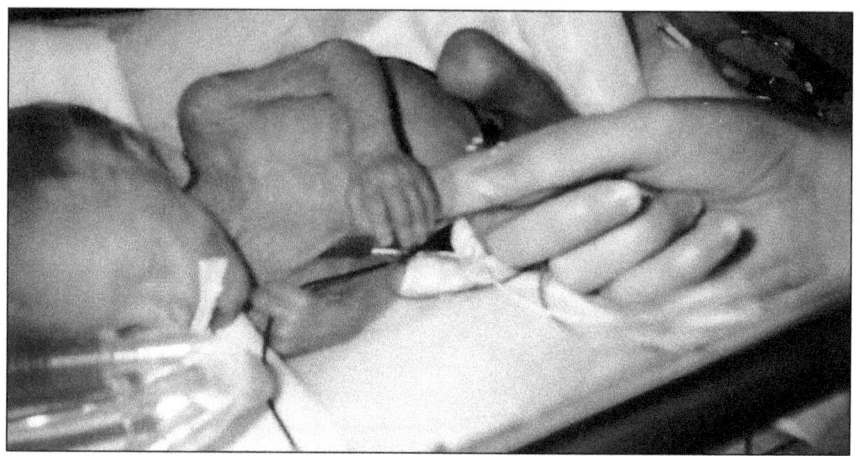

This is Ryan just forty-eight hours after he was born. He's holding my finger.

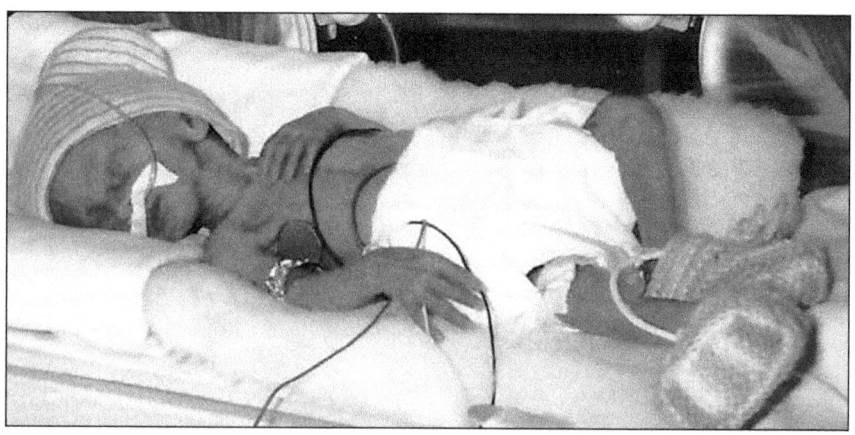

This photo shows Ryan at about two weeks old. He is wearing his daddy's wedding ring around his arm.

*Photo Gallery*

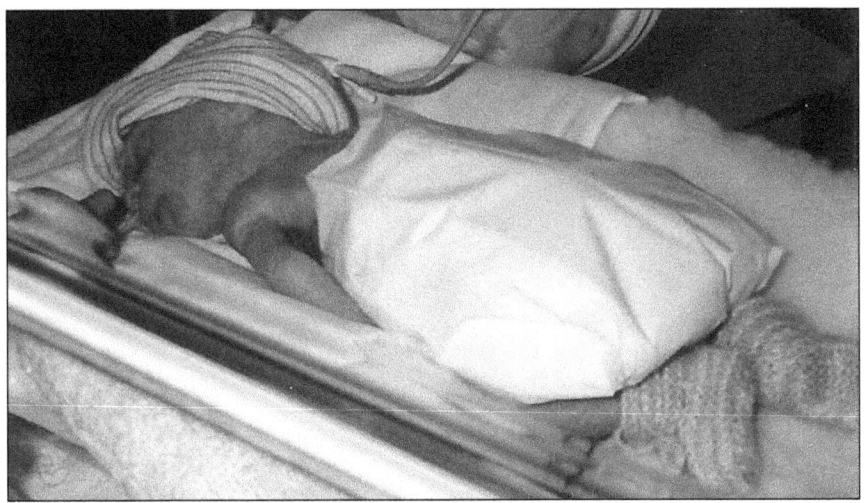

Ryan is wearing a preemie-sized diaper and booties that were twice as big as his feet.

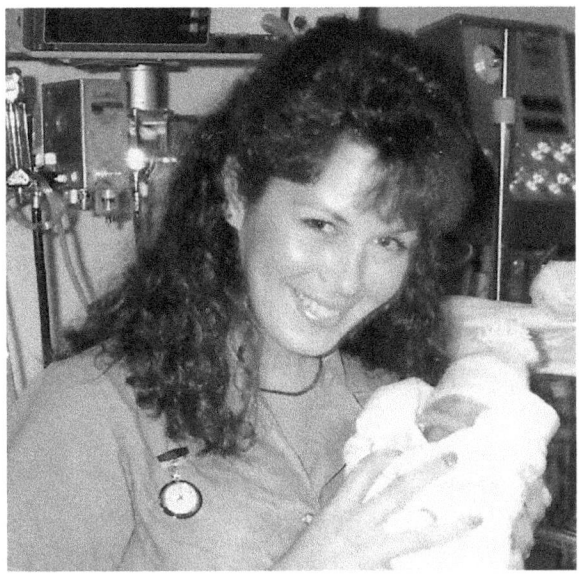

Ryan is three weeks old, and the first time out of his isolette. Nurse Pam is holding him, and he doesn't like the bright lights, so he's covering his eyes.

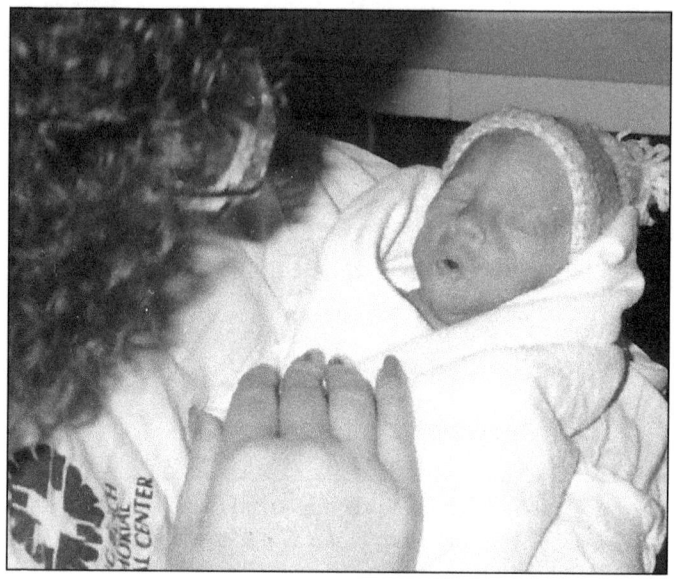

This is the first time I got to hold my baby boy.

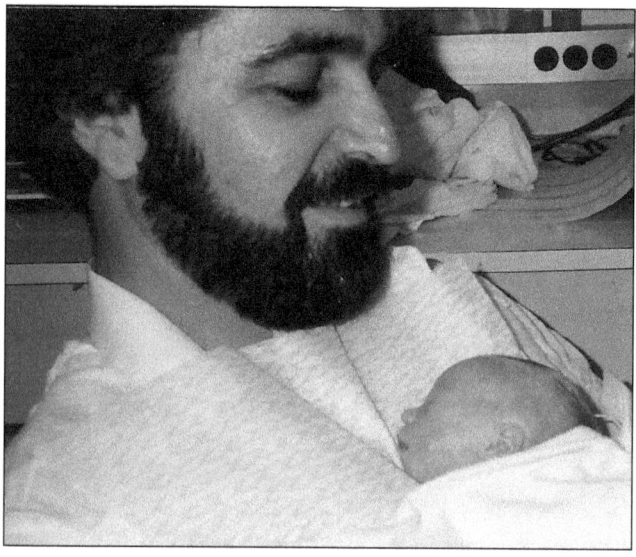

Kangaroo Care with daddy

*Photo Gallery*

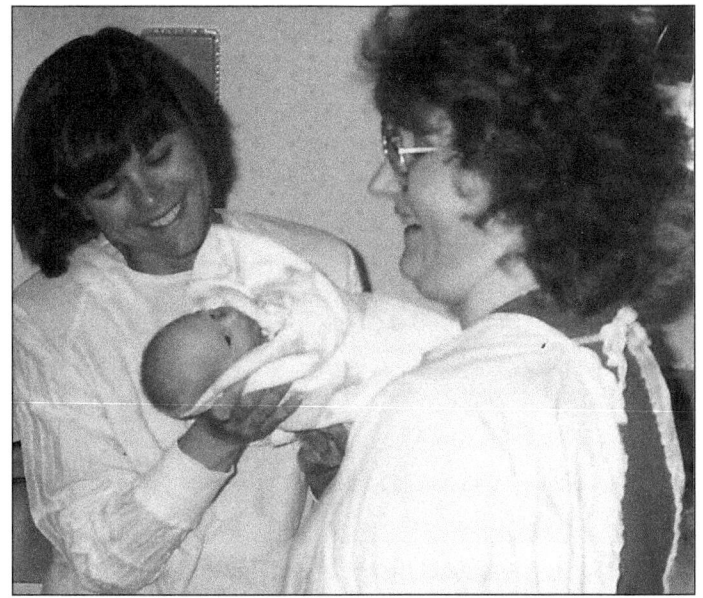

"Ryan, look at mommy." Ryan was able identify my voice over that of a stranger.

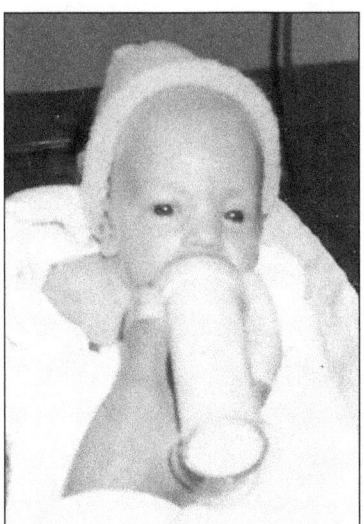

This is the size of the bottles they used at the NICU. It held two ounces.

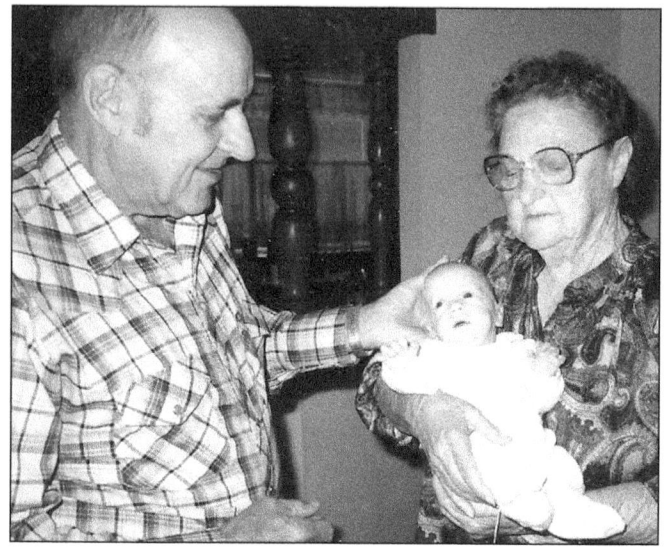

Ryan got to meet his great-grandpa and great-grandma Bickerstaff when he got home.

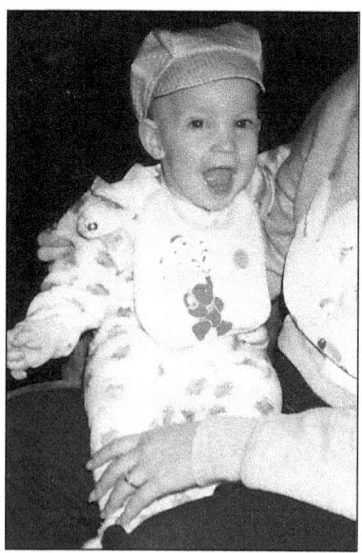

This was Ryan's permanent demeanor as a baby...and an adult.

*Photo Gallery*

Ryan with Daddy during his first trip to the beach.
He didn't like the sand on his feet.

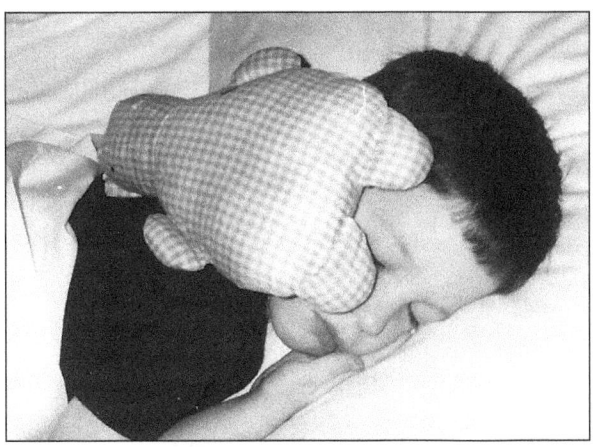

Ryan had a blue and white gingham check bunny named Bujie from the time he came home from the hospital. We sealed it in a plastic bag when he was about ten. It's dirty and stained, but I'm afraid to wash it because it might fall apart. Bujie went everywhere Ryan went. We even had to go back to a hotel and rescue him from under the covers when Ryan was four years old

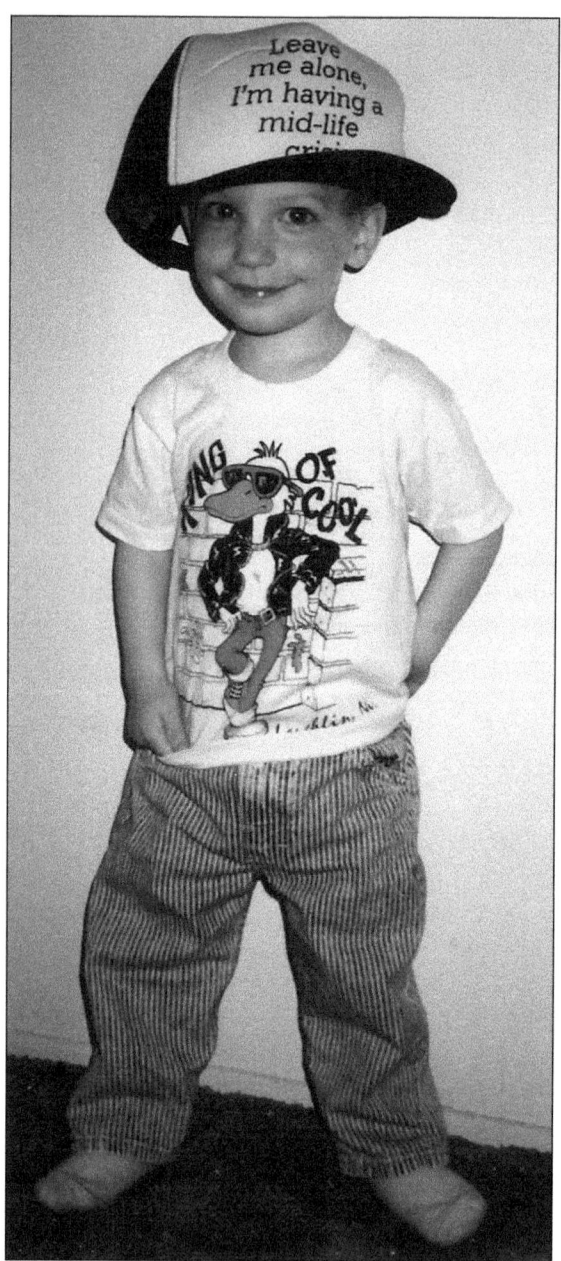

Ryan's shirt says "King of Cool" and his hat says, "Leave me alone. I'm having a mid-life crisis." Mike got the hat at his 40th over-the-hill birthday party.

*Photo Gallery*

This is my Aunt Sharon. She was
one of Ryan's blood donors.

Samantha is born! Ryan's t-shirt says,
"Bestest Big Brother" And he is.

Ryan loved to hold his baby sister.

Ryan loved to hold his baby sister while being held by his mom.

*Photo Gallery*

Ryan loved to hold his baby sister in a bucket...I sense a theme here.

Ryan's first computer. He got it when he was in Kindergarten.

We started Ryan on piano lessons when he was six years old. He prefers trumpet over piano.

Ryan and Sam both performed in Biola University's "Music Man". Biola had a great youth theater arts program. This was Ryan's third play. He also played in "School House Rock" at Biola and "Charlie and the Chocolate Factory" at the La Habra Civic Theater.

*Photo Gallery*

Ryan got a golden retriever puppy when he graduated from Kindergarten. Goldie was a member of our family for twelve years.

This family photo was taken on Thanksgiving in 1998.

Ryan poses with Nee and Papa before his 8th grade graduation.

Ryan and Samantha marched in the same parade when he was in high school and she was in middle school in 2006

Ryan's high school graduation picture, 2011.

The kids pose for a picture while vacationing in the Caribbean.

Ryan poses with his horn before his graduation from Dixie State College with an AS degree.

This photo is one of Ryan's favorites. While attending a music educator's conference in January of 2013 he got this picture with trumpet player Allen Vizutti. Then Mr. Vizutti was kind enough to autograph it for him.

www.ingramcontent.com/pod-product-compliance
Ingram Content Group UK Ltd.
Pitfield, Milton Keynes, MK11 3LW, UK
UKHW022212230426
12048UKWH00016BA/804